D0007339

501 Reasons Why Grandparents Know Best

501 Reasons Why Grandparents Know Best

EDITED BY
Ellen Kent and Beth Stephens

BARNES
&NOBLE
B O O K S
NEW YORK

The editors wish to express their gratitude to
Glorya Hale for helping to make this book
possible.

Thanks to Lucy Doyle
E.K.

2003 Barnes & Noble Books

ISBN 0-7607-4960-4

Text design by Rhea Braunstein

Printed and bound in the United States of America

03 04 05 06 07 08 09 MP 9 8 7 6 5 4 3 2 1

BVG

Contents

Contents

Contents

501 Reasons Why Grandparents Know Best

Great Things About Grandparents

Grandparents turn a deaf ear to
things you do wrong.

They always think you were the best
in the school play.

Grandparents always have time
to listen.

@ @ @

They have the best ice-cream flavors,
like Chocolate Chip Mint or Peanut
Butter and Jelly Fudge Ripple.

@ @ @

They always send you something
when you lose a tooth.

Grandparents give the best hugs—
bear hugs, good-bye hugs, "don't cry"
hugs, and hugs for no reason at all
except that they love you.

Grandparents will take you to
whatever movie you choose.

They never get tired of playing war or gin rummy.

They turn off their hearing aids when having dinner with your parents.

They will watch reruns of *Mister Rogers* with you.

Grandparents will watch reruns of *Mister Rogers* with you.

Grandparents will never forget to
bring you a rock for your collection.

They know *their* parents' and
grandparents' family histories.

Grandparents make the best fresh
lemonade.

Grandparents always have old newspaper clippings of historic events, like the first walk on the moon or President Kennedy's assassination.

⊙   ⊙   ⊙

They will always say hello to your imaginary friend.

They seem to sense your need to be
your own person long before your
parents do.

Grandparents will play hangman with
you during a rainstorm.

They have lived in the same house or
apartment forever.

Grandparents know how to make
great games out of nothing more than
paper and a pencil.

They can tell you about the bad
things your mom or dad did at
your age.

Grandparents are honored to bird-sit
your first parakeet when you go on
vacation.

They can identify family members in
old photos.

Their home smells like spices, vanilla,
and home-cooked meals.

Grandparents never sniff at
your ideas.

⊚   ⊚   ⊚

They always have basements and
attics filled with old treasures.

⊚   ⊚   ⊚

Grandparents are able to turn a
frown upside down, or a grumble
into a giggle.

Grandparents Around the World

Grandfather/Grandmother (English)

Bedstefader/Bedstemoder (Danish)

Opa or *Grootvader/*
Oma or *Grootmoeder* (Dutch)

Isoisä/Isoäiti (Finnish)

Grand-père/Grand-mère (French)

Grossvater/Grossmutter (German)

Pappous/Gigia (Greek)

Nagyapa/Nagyanya (Hungarian)

Nonno/Nonna (Italian)

Ojiisan/Obaasan (Japanese)

Bapîr/Bapêr (Kurdish)

Tipuna tane/Tipuna wahine (Maori)

Bestefar/Bestemor (Norwegian)

Dziadek/Babka (Polish)

Avô/Avó (Portuguese)

Bunic/Bunică (Romanian)

Dyed/Babushka (Russian)

Starý otec/Stará mama (Slovak)

501 Reasons Why Grandparents Know Best

Abuelo/Abuela (Spanish)

Farfar/Farmor (Swedish)

Büyükbaba/Büyükanne (Turkish)

Jadd i amjad/Naani (Urdu)

Seide/Bobe (Yiddish)

Grand Things About Grandmas

Grandma always seems to have a
never-ending candy bowl.

She shares stories of what your
grandfather was like when he
was young.

Grandma knows food heated on the
stove is better than food heated in
the microwave.

She knits the best sweaters.

She passes on her funky vintage
jewelry and dresses to you.

When Grandma makes yucky brussels sprouts for dinner, she always makes sure to prepare you a separate plate of your favorite dish—macaroni and cheese.

She knows how to make long car rides fun.

Grandma will put out cookies for your imaginary tea party.

She knows the casts and plots of all those great black-and-white movies.

Grandma lets you have chocolate cake or french fries for breakfast.

She will rub your feet when you're sick.

Grandma will let you try on her makeup and use her curlers.

Her cookies always have a special taste, but there is never a recipe.

You can count on Grandma to
gush over what a "beautiful girl"
or a "handsome young man"
you're becoming.

She still makes applesauce from
scratch and real rice pudding.

She gives the best hugs.

She lets you try on her wedding ring.

Grandma can turn an ordinary
Sunday-night dinner into a special
family event.

Grandma always seems to know
something is wrong just by looking
at your face.

She knows the secret to growing
beautiful roses.

She'll still seat you at the kid's table,
even though you're 34.

Grandma never fails to try and set you
up with "the nicest boy I met at Mrs.
Longstreet's barbecue."

A Grandmother Is . . .

A grandmother is a woman who is thrilled because her grandchild can recite the Gettysburg Address at eight when Lincoln couldn't do it until he was much older.

Milton Berle, American comedian

Just about the time a woman thinks her work is done, she becomes a grandmother.

Author unknown

Time and trouble will tame an advanced young woman, but an advanced old woman is uncontrollable by any earthly force.

Dorothy Sayers, British mystery writer

You're old enough to be a grandmother if you decide to find a job and discover the references on your last résumé are all deceased.

Mary McBride, author of Grandma Knows Best But No One Ever Listens!

🌀   🌀   🌀

If nothing is going well, call your grandmother.

Italian proverb

A grandmother will put a sweater on you when she is cold, feed you when she is hungry, and send you to bed when she is tired.

Erma Bombeck, American writer

and humorist

If your baby is "beautiful and perfect, never cries or fusses, sleeps on schedule, and burps on demand, an angel all the time" . . . you're the grandma.

Teresa Bloomingdale, American writer

The proliferation of support groups suggests to me that too many Americans are growing up in homes that do not contain a grandmother. A home without a grandmother is like an egg without salt.

Florence King, American writer and journalist

Grandmothers of every race and country have a legendary role as healers: Jewish grandmothers make chicken soup, others have their own remedies. When a child in a North American Yurok Indian tribe is ill, grandmother goes out into the wilderness to intervene with the spirits by singing and speaking to them. Every grandmother has her own songs.

Arthur Kornhaber, M.D., American
pediatrician and child psychiatrist

Let's bring back grandmothers—the old-fashioned kind, who take you by the hand and lead you into the future, safe and savvy and smarter than your mother.

Florence King, American writer and journalist

In many parts of the world, grandmothers are considered experts, and a young mother takes it for granted that when she has a question about her baby or needs a little help with him, she'll ask her mother.

Benjamin Spock, M.D., American pediatrician and writer

Of course there's such a thing as angels, only sometimes they don't have wings, and we call them grandmas.

Author unknown

ⓖ   ⓖ   ⓖ

A grandmother pretends she doesn't know who you are on Halloween.

Erma Bombeck, American writer and humorist

And so our mothers and grandmothers have, more often than not anonymously, handed on the creative spark, the seed of the flower they themselves never hoped to see—or like a sealed letter they could not plainly read.

Alice Walker, American writer

to grandpa

Grandmother: a wonderful mother with lots of practice.

Author unknown

A house needs a
grandma in it.

Louisa May Alcott, American writer

Uncles, and aunts, and cousins, are all very well, and fathers and mothers are not to be despised; but a *grandmother*, at holiday time, is worth them all.

Fanny Fern, American novelist, journalist, and feminist writer

Grandmas are moms with lots of frosting.

Author unknown

What in heaven's name is so strange about a grandmother dancing nude? I bet lots of grandmothers do it.

Sally Rand, American dancer and stripper

My grandmother remembers with her heart those tender childhood moments that I have long forgotten.

Author unknown

The unconditional love a grandmother gave a granddaughter when she was young may take on a renewed importance during the granddaughter's adulthood, especially when her decisions have more serious consequences and unqualified support is harder to find.

Hope Edelman, American writer

God couldn't be everywhere so He invented grandmothers.

Author unknown

Her grandmother, as she gets older, is not fading but rather becoming more concentrated.

Paulette Bates Alden, American writer

A grandmother is a baby-sitter who watches the kids instead of the television.

Author unknown

If you would civilize a man, begin with his grandmother.

Victor Hugo, French poet, playwright, and novelist

Even now I am not old, I never think of it, yet I am a grandmother to eleven children. I also have seventeen great-grandchildren, that's aplenty!

Grandma Moses (Anna Mary Robertson Moses), American painter

ⓖ　　ⓖ　　ⓖ

It's such a grand thing to be a mother of a mother—that's why the world calls her grandmother.

Author unknown

Grand Things About Grandpas

Grandpa knows the best way to tie
a tie.

⑥　　⑥　　⑥

He will get you the BB gun, pet rabbit,
or puppy that your parents won't.

Grandpa will give you candy to keep
you busy during church.

He always knows a good joke, how to
snatch your nose, and the trick to
pulling a penny from behind your ear.

He is a skilled fisherman and a very
relaxed driving teacher.

He'll build you your first dollhouse.

Grandpa can tell you his stories of
fighting in World War II.

He's always really interested in your
stamp collection.

When you sleep over, Grandpa
lets you stay up late to watch the
scary movie.

He will let you touch the elephants at
the zoo and won't even make you
wash your hands afterward.

Grandpa always makes sure you get
to blow out the candles after dinner.

He is the best keeper of a
cranky baby.

Grandpa will let you sit in the car and
pretend to drive.

A Grandfather Is . . .

A grandfather is a man who can't understand how his idiot son has such brilliant children.

Milton Berle, American comedian

ⓖ   ⓖ   ⓖ

Grandfathers impart information, ethics, and values that children learn nowhere else.

Arthur Kornhaber, M.D., American pediatrician and child psychiatrist

Grandfathers are less concerned with pregnancy problems than grandmothers. They are usually glad this is happening to some other man's wife.

Tom Buck, author of But Dad!

You've got to do your own growing, no matter how tall your grandfather was.

Irish proverb

Old Man: You get old and you can't do anybody any good any more.

Boy: You do me some good, Grandpa. You tell me things.

Robert Penn Warren, American novelist and poet

Perhaps the most important role for grandfathers to play today is that of models—
models of warm, caring, concerned, and
involved men who can serve as a vital reminder that *real men care for their families.*

Ruth K. Westheimer, German-born American
psychotherapist and writer

(9   (9   (9

There are fathers who do not love their children; there is not a grandfather who does not
adore his grandson.

Victor Hugo, French poet, playwright,
and novelist

One of the most powerful handclasps is that of a new grandbaby around the finger of a grandfather.

Author unknown

Grandfathers today are beginning to understand that their role affords them an opportunity to be with children—something that this new generation of grandfathers had little time for in their younger days.

> *Arthur Kornhaber, M.D., American*
> *pediatrician and child psychiatrist*

ⓖ   ⓖ   ⓖ

Every generation revolts against its fathers and makes friends with its grandfathers.

> *Lewis Mumford, American social philosopher*
> *and historian*

Somehow I have the feeling that if a grand-father became an astronaut, on his return, the grandchildren would ask, "What did you bring us?"

Milton Berle, American comedian

Grandchildren don't make a man feel old; it's the knowledge that he's married to a grandmother.

Author unknown

Grandfathers have seen it all. The wars and the weapons of war. The hurts and the harms of hate. Grandfathers hope for us. Wish for us. Sing our song. Cross their fingers that they were good fathers. Cross their fingers that they will be better "grandfathers."

Nikki Giovanni, American poet and activist

Things That Grandparents Understand That No One Else Does

That TVs today have too many channels

Early-bird specials

The endless fascination of family
photo albums

Saving used shopping bags and
wrapping paper "just in case"

Bedtime at 8:30—in separate beds

Corsets and pomade and other
strange things

Castor oil and salt water as cure-alls

The importance of good manners

Money based on a silver standard

What it was like not to have
air-conditioning

"Courtships"

Grandparent Fun Facts

The grandparent/grandchild relationship is second in emotional importance only to the parent/child relationship.

The 1990 United States census found that 5.5 percent of children under the age of 18 live in a grandparent-headed home.

The percentage was 3.2 percent in 1970.
Of the 2.3 million grandparents raising
grandchildren, nearly 1.5 million are
grandmothers.

Jack Shea and Jim Shea Jr. are the first
grandfather-grandson pair to win Olympic
gold medals (Jack in 1932 for speed skating;
Jim in 2002, seventy years later, for
skeleton). Up until his death in February
2002, Jack Shea was the oldest living
Olympic gold medal winner.

More than 70 percent of middle-aged and older people will become grandparents. A considerable number of grandparents will live long enough to become great-grandparents—and some will even become great-great-grandparents.

Today's grandmothers don't sit in rocking chairs anymore. In 1981, grandmother Barbara Wiedner started Grandmothers for Peace International after becoming concerned about the safety of her grandchildren from nuclear weapons.

Currently, this nonprofit organization has members and supporters across the nation and around the world.

Some research shows that as many as 9 out of 10 adult grandchildren feel their grandparents influenced their values and behaviors. With the increase in longevity, more children are really getting to know their grandparents.

The older population itself is getting older. In 1999, the 65 to 74 age group (18.2 million) was eight times larger than in 1900, the 75 to 84 group (12.1 million) was 16 times larger, and the 85-plus group (4.2 million) was 34 times larger.

Although the average age for becoming a grandparent is 50 years for women and a couple of years older for men, today's grandparents may range in age from 30 to 110. Grandchildren range from newborns to retirees.

Most grandparents have an average of 5 or 6 grandchildren.

Because of divorce and remarriage, many children have 6 to 8 adults in the "grandparent" role in their lives. Between 20 and 25 percent of grandparents will be step-grandparents either through their own or their adult children's divorces and remarriages.

One of the houses in Barbra Streisand's California compound is called "Grandma's House," and is decorated in New England family style.

In some cases, parents deny grandparents access to grandchildren. Grandparent rights have received increasing attention. Although no state grants an automatic right to visitation, the majority of states have enacted laws that promote grandparent visitation when it's found to be in a child's best interest.

As a special hello during her performances, comedian Carol Burnett always pulled on her ear to send her love to her grandmother.

There are about 70 million grandparents in the United States today, and each month 75,000 Americans 45 to 69 years old join the club. The number of grandparents is expected to grow to 80 million by 2010.

Heidi lived with her grandfather.

The "S" in Harry S. Truman stands for his grandfathers, Anderson Shipp Truman and Solomon Young.

What Experts Have to Say

Nothing is more helpful to a family with young children than a supportive grandparent, and few things cause more unhappiness than a tense parent-grandparent relationship.

Benjamin Spock, M.D., American pediatrician and writer

ⓖ   ⓖ   ⓖ

Grandparents who want to be truly helpful will do well to keep their mouths shut and their opinions to themselves until these are requested. At that point, if their ideas can be discussed—not as formed opinions but as suggestions to be taken or disregarded—they can be helpful.

T. Berry Brazelton, M.D., American pediatrician and child-development expert

ⓖ   ⓖ   ⓖ

The very fact that you don't look or act or feel like the grandparents of even a generation ago does not mean that you are less, but that you are more—in effect, an evolved form of grandparents, primed to do a bigger and more challenging job than any group before you.

Arthur Kornhaber, M.D., American
pediatrician and child psychiatrist

As a psychotherapist for thirty years I have heard many of my adult patients say, "I would never have made it without my grandparents."

Lillian Carson, American social worker, psychotherapist, and writer

ⓖ   ⓖ   ⓖ

Grandchildren and grandparents can fulfill a powerful need in each other to be listened to, to have one's thoughts and ideas taken seriously, and to be cherished with few if any demands placed upon each other, except to be.

Mary Cerney, Ph.D., American psychologist

When [children] are young, their way of operating with a grandparent is through example and non-verbal adoration that's not complicated by the psychological baggage that parents and kids have.

Arthur Kornhaber, M.D., American
pediatrician and child psychiatrist

Because grandparents do not have primary responsibility for their grandchildren's development, they have a special role—to love their grandchildren "no matter what . . ."

Bernice Weissbourd, president and
fellow of Family Focus, Inc.

6

The grandparents' job is to
give their grandchildren roots
and wings.

Lillian Carson, American social worker,

psychotherapist, and writer

6

Glance in the mirror, and you see a person who doesn't "look like a grandparent." But listen to your inner urges and you will find that your "grandparent hunger," your biological need to be a grandparent and to do the best possible job in that vital role, is as insistent as it has been for all people in all places and in all times.

Arthur Kornhaber, M.D., American pediatrician and child psychiatrist

6   6   6

Grandparents' Advice

"You should always drive at least ten miles per hour under the speed limit."

"Early to bed, early to rise . . ."

"A colored tennis ball perched on
your car antenna will help you find
your car in any shopping mall
parking lot."

"Plastic on the couch will keep it
clean for company."

"Dinner should be served no later
than 5:30."

"A hula hoop keeps your waistline
thin."

"A little nip of brandy will make you
feel better."

"A telephone call is always better
than an e-mail."

"The only cure for a cold is
chicken soup."

"A cup of warm milk will help you go
to sleep."

"Save your pennies for a rainy day."

"A small CD player should cost less
than a large CD player, not more."

"TV dinners are no substitute for a
real meal."

"Udder balm is the best thing for
skin rashes."

"Carry an extra sweater. It might
get cold."

Grandparents Day

The idea for a Grandparents Day was conceived in 1970 by Marian Lucille Herndon McQuade, a West Virginia housewife with 40 grandchildren and eight great-grandchildren.

The official flower of Grandparents Day is the forget-me-not.

The first Grandparents Day was proclaimed in 1973 in West Virginia by Governor Arch Moore. Also in 1973, Senator Jennings Randolph of West Virginia introduced a Grandparents Day resolution in the United States Senate.

Hallmark Cards requested permission from the McQuades to publish greeting cards for the holiday, volunteering a royalty to defray expenses. However, the McQuades declined the royalty, saying, "It would take away from the [day's] meaning."

Grandchildren can nominate their grandparents for the National Grandparents of the Year Award through the National Grandparents Day Council. There is a winner for every state, and past prizes have included trips and computers.

September was chosen for the holiday to signify the autumn years of life.

The proclamation of National Grandparents Day was signed by President Jimmy Carter, citing it as a day "to honor grandparents, to give grandparents an opportunity to show love for their children's children, and to help children become aware of the strength, information, and guidance older people can offer."

Best Gifts for Grandparents

Secret Agent Walking Stick: This cane is loaded with gadgets, including a built-in flashlight, red reflector safety light, and a secret pill compartment.

Golf Ball Retriever: With a reach of more than 6 feet, this wand helps retrieve errant golf balls from sand and water traps.

Red Garden Scooter: Takes the kneeling out of gardening with a 360° swiveling seat perched atop tractor-style wheels.

Stock Quote Magnifier: Grandparents can check their millions with this small dome that magnifies that tiny print four times.

Leather Brag Book: With room for plenty of 4-by-6 pics, any grandparent can tote along his or her pride and joy in style.

The Joy of Grandchildren

Grandchildren are so much fun, I should have had them first.

> *Lois Wyse, American advertising*
> *executive and writer*

The handwriting on the wall means the grandkids have found the crayons.

> *Author unknown*

I would, believe me, go into the coffin with a smile on my face to have seen and held on my lap a couple of grandchildren.

Dan Greenberg, author of
How to Be a Jewish Mother

ⓖ　　ⓖ　　ⓖ

The glow of attending Grandparents Day lingers for a long time. It's heady stuff to have your grandson walk you down to the boiler room and introduce you to the custodian.

Mary McBride, author of Grandma Knows
Best But No One Ever Listens!

The best gift I can give my father is to bring my daughter to visit him. She touches his foot, and he wiggles his toes. She throws a ball at him; he throws it back. She smiles a beatific smile. She kisses his hand and his cheek. She waves bye-bye. She has no words for this. It is pure love.

Garrison Keillor, American writer and humorist

Perfect love sometimes does not come until the first grandchild.

Welsh proverb

Our grandchildren accept us for ourselves, without rebuke or effort to change us, as no one in our entire lives has ever done, not our parents, siblings, spouses, friends—and hardly ever our own grown children.

Ruth Goode, American writer

ⓖ   ⓖ   ⓖ

A mother becomes a true grandmother the day she stops noticing the terrible things her children do because she is so enchanted with the wonderful things her grandchildren do.

Lois Wyse, American advertising executive and writer

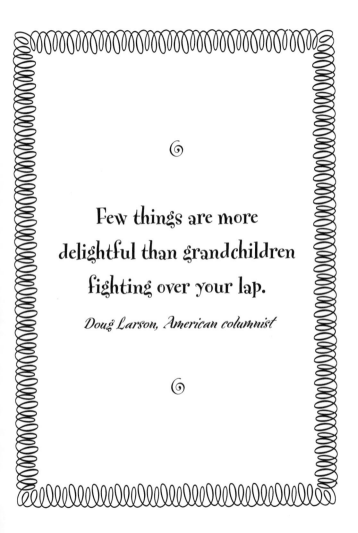

Few things are more
delightful than grandchildren
fighting over your lap.

Doug Larson, American columnist

Dearer than our children are the children of our children.

Egyptian proverb

Together you and the children who are very special to you can visit enchanted lands—of good fairies, and some who are wicked, of handsome princes and beautiful princesses, of dwarfs and giants, of magic spells and wondrous imaginings—and share moments that will become their golden memories.

Glorya Hale, American editor and writer

Grandchildren are a renewal of life, a little bit of us going into the future.

Helene Schellenberg Barnhart,
American writer

If I had no other interruptions in my work than my grandson, that would be more than enough, but I get so much pleasure from it. He follows me everywhere, like a chicken following a hen.

Alessandra de'Machingi Strozzi, fifteenth-
century Italian householder and letter writer

Grandchildren are wonderful, but nothing is more embarrassing than having to beg your ten-year-old granddaughter to help you program your new computer.

Ted Krause, American columnist

Never have children, only grandchildren.

Gore Vidal, American novelist and essayist

Greatness of name in the father ofttimes overwhelms the son; they stand too near one another. The shadow kills the growth so much, that we see the grandchild come more and oftener to be the heir to the first.

Samuel Johnson, English lexicographer, critic, and conversationalist

⑥　　⑥　　⑥

Holding a great-grandchild makes getting old worthwhile.

Author unknown

Grandchildren help us
remember that we
once were kids.

Clarice Orr, American writer

Each new grandchild, each brood of grand-children, can be a fresh delight, a deeply satisfying reward for the long years of parenthood.

Margaret Mead, American anthropologist and writer

[He] is a mighty fine grandson, smart as you find them. I expect him to be United States Senator by the time he is forty.

Sam Ealy Johnson, about his three-year-old grandson, Lyndon Johnson

Grandparents are frequently more congenial with their grandchildren than with their children. An old man, having retired from active life, regains the gaiety and irresponsibility of childhood. He is ready to play. . . . [H]e cannot run with his son, but he can totter with his grandson. Our first and last steps have the same rhythm; our first and last walks are similarly limited.

André Maurois, French writer and critic

Not all of us think grandkids are the great-est—but that was before I met mine.

Jane Russell, American actor

Grandchildren are the perfect excuse for us to buy stuff we couldn't afford for our own children or we won't buy for ourselves.

Clarice Orr, American writer

Posterity is the patriotic name for grandchildren.

Art Linkletter, American humorist

⑥   ⑥   ⑥

The reason grandparents and grandchildren get along so well is that they have a common enemy.

Sam Levenson, American humorist and writer

⑥   ⑥   ⑥

Grandchildren provide an avenue that leads us right into life. With them we experience life unfolding. Their fresh view not only delights us but awakens us to new possibilities. It's refreshing. It's healthy. It keeps us young. It is the joy of grandparenting.

Lillian Carson, American social worker,
psychotherapist, and writer

Grandchildren are God's reward for growing old.

Proverb

501 Reasons Why Grandparents Know Best

By the time the youngest children have learned to keep the house tidy, the oldest grandchildren are on hand to tear it to pieces.

Christopher Morley, American writer

They say genes skip generations. Maybe that's why grandparents find their grandchildren so likeable.

Author unknown

Children's children are the crown of old men.

Psalm 17:6

❦

My grandmother and my
mother live on through my
daughter as surely as they live
on in me. . . . They are her
inspiration. She is their song.

Hope Edelman, American writer

❦

My granddaughter came to spend a few weeks with me, and I decided to teach her to sew. After I had gone through a lengthy explanation of how to thread the machine, she stepped back, put her hands on her hips, and said in disbelief, "You mean you can do all that, but you can't operate my Game Boy?"

Author unknown

Grandparent Superlatives

Biggest Gift From a Grandmother: A 400-pound, steel-reinforced concrete star embedded with rocks. Chloe Bell began collecting rocks from the 48 states in the 1930s. She wrote to people all over the country, asking them to send local rocks, and her son made her the star from her collection. He kept it after her death and is about to give it to her grandson.

Most Prolific Grandmother: According to *The Guinness Book of World Records,* 123-year-old Malan Devi, who died in her village of Wazidiwal in northwestern India, was survived by a 182-member family, which includes sons, daughters, grandsons, and granddaughters.

Most Prolific Grandfather: According to Guinness, Samuel S. Mast, who died in

October 1992, had 824 living descendents
from his 11 children, including great-great
grandchildren.

Youngest Grandmother: According to Ripley's
Believe It or Not!, Mum Zi, a member of Chief
Akkiri's harem on the island of Calabar in
Nigeria, became a grandmother when she was
17 years old. Her daughter was eight years old.

Youngest Grandfather: Dale Wright of
Warwickshire, England, who was 29 when
his granddaughter was born.

Highest-Flying Grandfathers: *Atlantis* shuttle astronauts Jerry Ross and Lee Morin, nicknamed the Silver Team, took the first spacewalk ever by two grandfathers on April 13, 2002. The 54-year-old Ross and the 49-year-old Morin each had two grandchildren at the time of their walk.

Best Vacation With a Grandparent: Disney World

Flashiest Grandmother: Tina Turner

Sexiest Grandfather: Paul Newman

Sexiest Grandmother: Sophia Loren

Most Rugged Grandfather: Clint Eastwood

Most Regal Grandmother: The Queen Mother

Most Artistic Grandmother: Grandma Moses

Gentlest Grandfather: Burl Ives

Hairiest Grandmother: Little Red Riding Hood's grandmother

Most Outspoken Grandmother: Eleanor Roosevelt

Being a Grandparent

Becoming a grandparent is a second chance. For you have a chance to put to use all the things you learned the first time around and may have made mistakes on. It's all love and no discipline. There's no thorn in this rose.

Joyce Brothers, American psychologist and columnist

I've never had a burning desire to be a grand-father, but now I feel it's one of life's greatest pleasures—feeling those little hands patting my face is pure ecstasy.

Walter Cronkite, American journalist

Let's face it. Baby-sitting is a bona fide occu-pational hazard of being a grandmother. Un-fortunately, you don't get workman's comp.

Mary McBride, author of Grandma Knows Best, But No One Ever Listens!

I wouldn't have found it so hard to go ahead with it if I had realized that having a baby was the only way I could ever become a grandmother.

Phyllis Diller, American comedian

to grandpa

I wanted to shout it to the world: I'm a Grandparent!!!!

Ruth K. Westheimer, German-born American psychotherapist and writer

A friend of mine was asked how she liked having her first great-grandchild. "It was wonderful," she replied, "until I suddenly realized that I was the mother of a grandfather!"

Robert L. Rice, M.D., American physician

The love between a grandparent and grandchild is unconditional. It's the simplest and least complicated intense human love bond. It's "I love you because you exist."

Arthur Kornhaber, M.D., American pediatrician and child psychiatrist

Grandmother . . . I will grasp and savor the true beauty of that word—its grandeur and its glory. To be a grandmother. What a compliment. May I live up to it.

Marjorie Holmes, American writer

I suddenly realized that through no act of my own I had become biologically related to a new human being.

Margaret Mead, American anthropologist
and writer

When you've held that first grandbaby you know continuity in life and that you must do right now so that grandbaby will do better later.

Ann Richards, American politician

I was blown away when I held Chad for the first time. I don't know if I was shell-shocked from realizing that my first-born was now a mother.

Allan Zullo, American writer

I tried to be cool about the looming first grandchild . . . but my unconscious tricked me into misreading the nameplate on a Pontiac as "Grand Ma" when it was clearly "Grand Am."

Anne Bernays, American writer

I thought I was in total control. I became insane. I was sure the baby's long fingers meant an absolutely brilliant career as a concert pianist.

Jack Lemmon, American actor

⊚   ⊚   ⊚

We have become a grandmother.
Margaret Thatcher, English politician and England's first female prime minister

One of the hardest things about being a grandparent is relinquishing control. We understand that we're not in charge anymore, but it's quite a transition to go from speaking our minds to biting our tongues.

Lillian Carson, American social worker,
psychotherapist, and writer

No cowboy was ever faster on
the draw than a grandparent
pulling a baby picture out
of a wallet.

Author unknown

When you become a grandparent, you can reinvent yourself. You can absolve yourself of all your failures as a parent and start all over when you're with your grandkids.

Perry Buffington, American family psychologist and syndicated columnist

To be a grandparent is to pierce the bull's-eye of eternity.

Alma Bond, American writer

If you see a book, a rocking chair, and a grandchild in the same room, don't pass up a chance to read aloud. Instill in your grandchildren a love of reading. It's one of the greatest gifts you can give.

Barbara Bush, American first lady

ⓖ   ⓖ   ⓖ

I dig being a mother . . . and of course, as a grandmother, I just run amok.

Whoopi Goldberg, American actor and comedian

The joy of becoming a mother was a prelude
to the joy of becoming a grandmother.

Author unknown

Grandparenting is one of the last adventures
I am going to experience, and I do not plan to
miss a moment of it.

Ruth K. Westheimer, German-born American
psychotherapist and writer

As I've gotten older, I've gotten more sure of myself. I was a shy and withdrawn young mother; and I am not a shy and withdrawn grandmother.

Author unknown

Grandmotherhood does not give us the right to speak without thinking, but only the right to think without speaking.

Lois Wyse, American advertising executive and writer

Being grandparents sufficiently removes us from the responsibilities so that we can be friends—really good friends.

Allan Frome, American writer

Soon I will be an old, white-haired lady, into whose lap someone places a baby, saying, "Smile, Grandma!"—I, who myself so recently was photographed on my grandmother's lap.

Liv Ullmann, Swedish actor

Because [grandparents] are usually free to love and guide and befriend the young without having to take daily responsibility for them, they can often reach out past pride and fear of failure and close the space between generations.

Jimmy Carter, 39th president of the United States

⑥   ⑥   ⑥

I wish to ask you how you find yourself, on being a grandfather. . . . The prospect is worse than the reality.

Marie de Rabutin-Chantal, Marquise de Sévigné, seventeenth-century French letter writer

Once your children are grown up and have children of their own, the problems are theirs, and the less the older generation interferes the better.

Eleanor Roosevelt, American writer and first lady

Surely, two of the most satisfying experiences in life must be those of being a grandchild or a grandparent.

Author unknown

Only take heed to thyself, and keep thy soul diligently, lest thou forget the things which thine eyes have seen, and lest they depart from thy heart all the days of thy life: but teach them to thy sons, and thy sons' sons.

Deuteronomy 4:9

If becoming a grandmother was only a matter of choice I should advise every one of you straightaway to become one. There is not fun for old people like it!

Hannah Whitall Smith, American writer,
evangelist, and pacifist

Becoming a grandmother is wonderful. One moment you're just a mother. The next you are all-wise and prehistoric.

Pam Brown, Australian poet and playwright

Grandparents' Specialties

Making cookies in special shapes

⑥ ⑥ ⑥

Teaching you how to fish

⑥ ⑥ ⑥

Turning off their hearing aids at
significant moments

Letting you help plant their garden

Multicolored Jell-O molds

Teaching you how to make
paper airplanes

Knowing when to spoil you and when
to scold you (but not too much)

Building dollhouses and tree houses

Baking bread and letting you help

A secret drawer with special "kid games"

Apple pie

Fun trips to the zoo and to the
amusement park

Black-and-white home movies of
family events from before you
were born

Teaching you the waltz and the cha-cha

Famous Grandparents and Grandchildren

John Barrymore and Drew Barrymore

Henry Fonda and Bridget Fonda

Michael Redgrave and Joely and
Natasha Richardson

John Francis Fitzgerald and John F. Kennedy

John D. Rockefeller Sr. and Nelson A. Rockefeller

Ernest Hemingway and Margaux and Mariel Hemingway

William Henry Harrison and Benjamin Harrison

Samuel Adams and John Quincy Adams

Baron Karl von Schlebrugg and
Uma Thurman

Ozzie Nelson and Matthew Nelson

Lon Chaney and Ron Chaney

The Queen Mother and Prince Charles

Other Famous "Grandparents"

Grandfather clock

Granny Smith apples

Grandfather clause

Granny glasses

Granny dress

Granny knot

Grammy Awards

The Famous on Their Grandparents

Our matriarch, Grandmother Page, was of wagon breed, a big woman of unsurpassed energy. She was up at three-thirty or four o'clock in the morning, to bake and churn and get ready for the fields. At night, along with the cooking and sewing, there was energy left for her reading.

Dan Rather, American television newscaster

Dear Grandmamma, with what we give,
We humbly pray that you may live
For many, many happy years.
Although you bore us all to tears.
Hilaire Belloc, British novelist and politician

6   6   6

My great-great-great-grandmother walked as a slave from Virginia to Eatonton, Georgia. . . . It is in memory of this walk that I chose to keep and to embrace my "maiden" name, Walker.

Alice Walker, American writer

We had an understanding, Grandma and I. She didn't treat me like a child and I didn't treat her like a mother.

Erma Bombeck, American humorist

and writer

Above all, she saw the funny side of life and we laughed until we cried—oh, how I shall miss her laugh and wonderful wisdom born of so much experience and an innate sensitivity to life. She was quite simply the most magical grandmother you could possibly have, and I was utterly devoted to her.

Prince Charles, on the Queen Mother

⊙   ⊙   ⊙

My kids just love Grandpa Arnold. . . . They love Grandpa Arnold because he gives them presents.

Steven Spielberg, American film director

Sofie Mann, born in the Ukraine, had raised me. Sofie seemed to have been born a grandmother. The photographs of her, beginning in her girlhood, show the same calm, ready dignity, the unconscious patience that never left her. . . . The photographs do not reveal her capacity for pranks and foolishness.

Barbara Myerhoff, American anthropologist

෧ ෧ ෧

My grandmother was older than any other grownup around me, which set her apart from them, and she didn't behave as they did. Specifically, she never assumed any authority over me. . . . I thought of her as another child like me, albeit rather old. She was ready to play draughts, go to the cinema, more or less whenever I wanted.

Nina Bawden, English novelist

෧ ෧ ෧

I loved my grandmother more than any other human being because she never lied, never told you what you wanted to hear, never compromised.

Roseanne Barr, American comedian and actor

Grandma always wanted to understand things, and she was willing to listen or read until she did. There was only one subject, she decided rather fastidiously, that she did not wish to pursue. That was birth control. At eighty, she said, she did not need to know about it.

Margaret Mead, American anthropologist and writer

There's a photograph of Nana in a Lucille Ball kind of dress and her hair spilling down, thick, dark, loose, curly, and that's when I see I am her. We both have hair like our souls, lively and unsettled.

Serena Makofsky, American writer

My grandparents thought I—as well as each of their other twenty-five grandchildren— was special.

Kathryn Zullo, American writer

She seems to have had the ability to stand firmly on the rock of her past while living completely and unregretfully in the present.

Madeleine L'Engle, American writer

ⓖ   ⓖ   ⓖ

So many things we love are you, I can't seem to explain except by little things, by flowers and beautiful handmade things—small stitches. So much of our reading and thinking—so many sweet customs and so much of our . . . well, our religion. It is all *you.* I hadn't realized it before. This is so vague, but do you see a little, dear Grandma? I want to thank you.

Anne Morrow Lindbergh, American writer,
poet, and aviator

She was the last of the generation of real grandmothers. One of the women who made a special grace of age.

Helen Hayes, American actor

Grandpa . . . was ever ready to cheer and help me, ever sure that I was a remarkable specimen.

Miles Franklin, Australian writer

She sees herself as a victim of her era when there were fewer options for women, especially those with a wild spirit and freedom in their eyes. I look at her and see success and inspiration. Her life is something I wish to touch, attempting to as I write, grabbing for a piece of her nomadic spirit.

Serena Makofsky, American writer

⊚   ⊚   ⊚

I could do no wrong in Gramma's eyes. Ever. I think that if I had wound up a serial killer instead of a musician, Gramma would still have loved me.

Barry Manilow, American musician

My grandmother raised eight children of her own and informally adopted several others [and] I always associated my family's openness, their willingness to help others in need with Gran's and my parents' strong religious faith. It was a living faith that guided every aspect of their lives.

Andrew Young, American civil rights activist,
congressman, and statesman

ⓖ   ⓖ   ⓖ

Gramsie filled much of the void left by my parents' careers.

Maureen Reagan, American writer

[My grandmother] was the strongest woman I ever knew, even though she stood less than five feet high.

Ralph Bunche, Nobel Peace Prize winner

My grandmother was one of the most kind and thoughtful people I have ever met in my life. Everyone who ever knew her felt her compassion and was impressed by her grace.

George W. Bush, 43rd president
of the United States

The first person ever to notice my music ability was not my father or my mother but Grandma Ada McGill back in Illinois. Grandma, who lived to be nearly a hundred, always remembered your name and recognized something about you, when somebody else might have needed a doggone scorecard to sort out all the children.

Barbara Mandrell, American entertainer

⑥　　⑥　　⑥

The ability to laugh is the greatest gift I could receive from my bigger-than-life grandmother.

Valerie Kack-Brice, American clinical
social worker

I have never met anyone who had quite the amazing force without effort that my grandmother possessed.

Ethel Barrymore, American actor

I never had the kind of grandmother who wore aprons and spectacles and pulled warm cookies from the oven, the kind who exists more often in children's books than in real life. . . . The grandmother I knew was color-ful, opinionated, ubiquitous, stubborn, lov-ing, patient, devoted, intelligent, funny, uncontrollably obsessive, wildly supersti-tious, and capable of both astonishing acts of compassion and unpredictable fits of rage.

Hope Edelman, American writer

6   *6*   *6*

My own grandmother was one of those un-
professional nurses who served without rec-
ompense, from the mere love of it, even
though she had a host of little children to
care for. . . . [My grandmother] was the unof-
ficial nurse for Back Creek residents as well
as for my own family, risking her own life to
help the sick and comfort the dying.

Willa Cather, American writer

I was always happy at Granny Scarberry's home. She was a tiny woman with bright-blue laughing eyes who was always fun to be with, and she showered my brother and me with affection and attention.

Chuck Norris, American actor

6   6   6

She never, ever moved slowly. Even in her nineties she was going like the speed of light. And her head stayed sharp—right up until she died, her daughter had to read the newspapers to her.

Margaret Truman Daniels, American writer

[My maternal grandmother] was sharply opinionated and took charge of each slight opportunity, edging herself into the fabric of our household.

Shirley Temple Black, American child star and stateswoman

Perhaps nothing is more valuable for a child than living with an adult who is firm and loving. My mother was trustworthy in all matters that involved our care. Grandma was trustworthy in quite a different way. She meant exactly what she said, always.

Margaret Mead, American anthropologist and writer

I knew Grandma believed in meeting reality head on. She once told me, "Baby, life just ain't fair."

Claudia Limbert, American university
president and writer

Grandmother, a.k.a. . . .

Grandma

Granny

Nana

Back-scratcher

World-class Cookie Maker

Nanny

The Matriarch

Crying-baby Soother

Quilt Maker

Flower Nurturer

Mamie

Grandfather, a.k.a. . . .

Grandpa

Gramps

Poppy

The Patriarch

501 Reasons Why Grandparents Know Best

Pop-Pop

Top Fly Fisherman

Official Turkey-carver

Best Storyteller

Granddad

Grandparent Fashion Trends

Bow ties

⑥　　⑥　　⑥

Pants pulled up to the chest

⑥　　⑥　　⑥

Orthopedic shoes

Wearing suspenders and a belt at the
same time

Old "pilly" sweaters

Housedresses with zippers up
the front

Blue hair and teased-up bouffants

"World's Greatest Grandpa" baseball
caps and T-shirts

Button-down cardigans

Support hose, usually rolled to
the knees

Girdles

Shawls

Fishing hats

Plastic rain hats

Pomade

Old Spice

Lessons Learned

My affection for Grandpa Alfonso goes beyond family ties and ethnic pride. More than anyone else, he showed me that with the right attitude and a little guts, life could be an adventure.

Al D'Amato, United States senator

It is said that persons have few teachable moments in their lives. Mamma seems to have caught me at each one I had between the age of three and thirteen.

Maya Angelou, American poet, writer,
and entertainer

⑥　　⑥　　⑥

If you want to know where I come by the passionate commitment I have to bringing people together without regard to race, it all started with my grandfather.

William J. Clinton, 42nd president
of the United States

It was my grandmother who most times fed us, and her spirit is always with us as a part of our own personalities (I hope). I loved my grandmother so much because she was Good, if that has any meaning in the world. She'd tell you, "Do unto others as you'd have them do unto you," and you knew that's what she believed and that's what she practiced.

Amiri Baraka (Leroi Jones), American poet,
writer, and publisher

ⓖ ⓖ ⓖ

The strength of my conscience came from Grandma, who meant what she said. Perhaps nothing is more valuable for a child than living with an adult who is firm and loving—and Grandma was loving.

Margaret Mead, American anthropologist
and writer

My grandmother taught me to believe in miracles.

Lilly Mary Vigil, American art gallery owner

My grandfather once told me that there are two kinds of people: those who do the work and those who take the credit. He told me to try to be in the first group; there was much less competition.

Indira Gandhi, Indian politician and former prime minister

Grandmother was essential. She shaped all of us, willy-nilly, so that we talked and ate more politely than we might have without her.

M. F. K. Fisher, American writer

In retrospect, as I have grown older, I have realized more and more the importance [my grandmother] had in molding my outlook on life. Her fearlessness, her public spirit, her contempt for convention, and her indifference to the opinion of the majority have always seemed good to me and have impressed themselves upon me as worthy of imitation.

Bertrand Russell, English mathematician and philosopher

What I learned from Grandma's stories was this: Women could do hard things and do them competently; problems could be worked out if you ignored what everyone else told you and did what the situation required.

Sue Hubbell, American writer and beekeeper

I use her as a role model . . . an intelligent and beautiful woman who led an interesting life in her own right.

Maria Shriver, American journalist

Grandma . . . had a great deal to do with the education of her granddaughters. In general she not so much trained as just shed herself upon us.

Bertha Damon, American writer

Grandma held our family together. She emanated a strength, drawing on her faith. She renewed our commitment to excel and do better.

Joseph Kennedy Jr., American politician

to grandpa

I cultivate
Being Uppity
It's something
My Gramom taught me.

Kate Rushin, American poet

Mysteries to Grandparents

VCRs

Computers

Grandchildren's music choices

Cell phones

Baggy pants

Buying fast food when you can make a better meal at home

The need for more than one TV in the house

New math

Athletes' salaries

Today's dating rituals

Grandma's and Grandpa's Favorite Expressions

"When I was your age . . ."

⑥   ⑥   ⑥

"My grandson/granddaughter can run/draw/speak faster/better/clearer than your grandson/granddaughter."

"They don't make it like they
used to."

"My, how you've grown!"

"Out of a can?"

"When you get to be my age . . ."

"Barbara, take a look at the adorable
picture I got of little Timmy the
other day."

"Retirement is overrated."

Fond Memories

Just as in Grandfather's courtroom, many women also gathered in my grandmother's domain, the kitchen, to pour out their troubles and joys, to voice their problems and difficulties.

Isaac Bashevis Singer, American writer of Yiddish literature

One of my most memorable lessons in gamesmanship came from my paternal grandfather. . . . One afternoon he left the table for the bathroom while I shuffled . . . I arranged the deck so the cards would be dealt in my favor . . . but . . . I had set up my grandfather for a quick and overwhelming victory. . . . Grandpa was not one to coddle a vanquished foe. "Whoo-boy! Am I killing you!" he laughed as he slapped down winning hands. I wanted to blurt, "You didn't win! I cheated!" But I seethed in silence, and learned to set up the cards better.

Patrick Boyle, editor of Youth Today

⑥　　⑥　　⑥

Even when my grandfather sat in his salmon upholstered lounge chair and trapped me between his crossed ankles, refusing to release me until I said the magic words, *Open sesame,* I never felt the desperate need to escape.

Hope Edelman, American writer

My earliest recollections of the country were gained on short walks with my grandfather when I was perhaps not over three years old.

John Muir, Scottish-born American naturalist

I still see Nana after every Sunday dinner trying to divide her lemon meringue pie into nine perfectly equal pieces.

Carolyn J. Fairweather Hughes, American poet

[My grandmother] was always a very old lady to me. I remember she got an old-age pension of eighteen dollars a month, and occasionally the family had to borrow money from her.

Charles Schultz, American cartoonist

On her seventy-fifth birthday, [my grandmother] played softball with her grandsons on the beach, and took pride in hitting home runs into the ocean.

Gloria Steinem, American writer, activist, and journalist

Every Sunday my grandmother Selma would take me to the park where we would meet her sister and other friends who had brought their grandchildren. I think I inherited the talkativeness that has served me so well in my career from Grandma Selma. She was a wonderful presence in my life.

Ruth K. Westheimer, German-born American psychotherapist and writer

I doubt that Grandma Page went beyond the sixth grade in school, and hers was not a home filled with books. . . . [S]he read aloud . . . from her precious copy of the Sears Roebuck catalog about garden seed and other items of home interest. . . . [She] read me page after page from it. I don't remember that she ever ordered anything. The Sears catalog was her dream book. Its content wasn't about garden seed. It was about her dreams.

Dan Rather, American television newscaster

The traditions of folklore and storytelling are strong in the West Indies, and in her musical patois my grandmother used to tell me vivid stories about vampires and other zombie stuff straight out of West Africa. Her stories taught me that behind me was something real and authentic and dignified, and this helped give me some feeling of self-worth as a child. I always had the feeling of pride in where I came from.

Kareem Abdul-Jabbar, American athlete

My grandmother thought my mother kept me under too much discipline and delighted in taking me to her cellar pantry and stuffing me with forbidden treats.

Russell Baker, American writer

I have a medallion my grandmother gave to my mother when she was a little girl, and which my mother in turn gave to me. . . . I don't go out without it, or if I do I am constantly aware of its absence and feel awkward, as if I had gone out in only my underwear. . . . Because it was hers, it is, to me, a talisman, a vital reminder of my real guardian angel, the one who played with me and sang with me, the one who taught me strength. . . .

Joanna Pashdag, American writer

⑥　　⑥　　⑥

When I was a youngster, I used to have to kneel and pray for long periods with my grandfather, who prayed aloud in an unintelligible mutter. One day I finally found the courage to tell him that I couldn't understand a word of his prayers. My grandfather slowly lifted up his head and looked at me with disdain. "I wasn't talking to you," he retorted.

Bill Cosby, American humorist and actor

Under [my grandfather's] reign, you had to eat everything on your plate, or sit at the dinner table until you did. You had to go to church, every Sunday. You had to sit up straight. ("Father laid down the law," said my mother. And I could picture him laying it down, on the dining-room table, in the form of two great slabs, like those toted around by Moses; only his were of wood.)

Margaret Atwood, Canadian writer

It was dramatic to watch my grandmother decapitate a turkey with an ax the day before Thanksgiving. Nowadays, the expense of hiring grandmothers for the ax work would probably qualify all turkeys so honored with "gourmet" status.

Russell Baker, American writer

Grandpa . . . was a tall, skinny, silent, grim black man who had fought in the Civil War with the Union Army. When he was angry he gritted his teeth with a terrifying, grating sound. He kept his army gun in his room, standing in a corner, loaded. He was under the delusion that the war between the states would be resumed.

Richard Wright, American writer

When I finally met my Grandma Val, I was eleven years old and she was everything the wood smoke that clung to her letters had promised. With her straight gray hair cut short like a man's, her fingers stained with nicotine, she was nothing like a grandmother was supposed to be: she was not powdered, coifed and soft; she smoked, drank, swore, wore pants, and told funny stories. I was utterly enthralled.

Louise Freeman-Toole, American writer
and photographer

I loved their home. Everything
smelled older, worn but safe;
the food aroma had baked
itself into the furniture.

Susan Strasberg, American actor and writer

When we grandchildren were all gathered around the solemn Sunday dinner table bored out of our minds with grown-up talk but not allowed to be excused, when no other adult was watching, eyes twinkling [my grandmother] would quietly detach her upper bridge and roll it out on her tongue with three tiny false teeth riding on it, and as our eyes bugged out, we could hear her characteristic deep delighted chuckle. . . .

Susan Kenney, American writer and educator

When my grandmother . . . hangs up each Saturday night at the end of our long-distance conversation, I always worry that I have left out some critical question: about her dreams and premonitions, her parents' life in New Mexico before it became a state, her memories of herbs, foods, and prayers. . . . Each conversation is an inheritance; I go into the week feeling whole.

Demetria Martinez, American journalist
and novelist

Best Movie and TV Grandparents

Grampa Abraham J. Simpson,
The Simpsons

Agnes Moorehead as Endora,
Bewitched

Irene Ryan as Granny,
Beverly Hillbillies

Grandmother Lulu Pickles,
The Rugrats

Will Geer as Grandpa Zeb Walton and
Ellen Corby as Grandma Esther Walton,
The Waltons

Nancy Marchand as Livia Soprano,
The Sopranos

Al Lewis as Grandpa Munster,
The Munsters

Grandpa Jones, *Hee Haw*

Katherine Helmond as Mona
Robinson, *Who's the Boss?*

Henry Fonda as Norman Thayer Jr.,
On Golden Pond

Jack Albertson as Grandpa Joe, *Willy
Wonka and the Chocolate Factory*

Peter Falk as The Grandfather,
The Princess Bride

What Grandparents Could Teach Parents (having had many years to gain perspective)

A nose ring isn't so bad in the grand scheme of things.

Holiday clothes are going to get dirty.

No prospective employer will be able
to find out what one's math grade was
in junior high school.

Coloring one's hair does not make it
disintegrate, and green and purple
hair eventually grows out.

Breaking curfew does not necessitate
alerting the National Guard.

A child can kiss a dog and not catch a
disease.

A young lady can get a good job even
if she has a tattoo.

Nobody ever died from eating too many jelly beans or not getting enough sleep.

"Just a little bit" of wine with dinner doesn't do any harm.

Things Grandparents Will Do for You That No One Else Will

Buy you that toy "just because"

⟳   ⟳   ⟳

Read you *three* books, not one,

before bedtime

Let you have a cookie just before
dinner

Scratch your back for as long as
you want

Let you set up a campsite in their
living room

Play cards with you for hours

Look at the blue frosting you put on
the cupcakes you made for them and
say, "Oh, how beautiful!"

Let you have a manicure for
kindergarten graduation

Buy you your 67th stuffed bear

Write you letters from their dog,
Skippy

Take you to an R-rated movie that
your parents would forbid

Let you eat all your Halloween candy
in one night

Send you gift-wrapped treats for
your cat

Always let you take the cherry off the
top of the fruit salad

Play Monopoly with you and let you
buy the best properties

Sing "I Love You Truly" to soothe you
at three o'clock in the morning after
you wake up from a nightmare

Not scream when they see your
pierced eyebrow

Let you pick the lily they have been
coaching to flower for six years

Save all your thank-you cards, local
newspaper clippings, and letters
from college

Let you watch horror movies late
at night

Send you cards for every holiday from Groundhog Day to Thanksgiving

⑥　　⑥　　⑥

Prepare your food the way you like it, even if it means cutting off the crusts of your PB&J and cutting grapes in half to remove the seeds

⑥　　⑥　　⑥

Rescue you from home and have
you stay over when Mom is being
"too strict"

Let you sleep in their bed, no matter
how old you are

Indulge your imagination by letting
you "cook" on the stove and hang
your doll clothes on the clothesline
to dry

Send you care packages with cookies
and "just in case" money while you're
in college

The Joy of Grandparents

No one . . . who has not known the inestimable privilege can possibly realize what good fortune it is to grow up in a home where there are grandparents.

Suzanne LaFollette, American politician, editor, and writer

ⓖ　　ⓖ　　ⓖ

A grandparent will accept your calls from anywhere—collect.

Erma Bombeck, American writer and humorist

Grandparents are given a second chance to enjoy parenthood with fewer of its tribulations and anxieties.

Margaret Mead, American anthropologist and writer

It didn't take me long to figure out that one of a grandparent's primary jobs is to always pretend there is very little a child can do that is bothersome.

John Rosemond, American family psychologist and syndicated columnist

The simplest toy, one that even the youngest child can operate, is called a grandparent.

Sam Levenson, American humorist and writer

From the outset, grandparents have one big advantage over parents. We're older and, hopefully, wiser.

Ruth K. Westheimer, German-born American psychotherapist and writer

Grandparents help kids understand and settle into a world that can be pretty confusing to newcomers.

Charles S. Slaybaugh, American writer

It is important for the elders to be willing to give wisdom and not to try to direct everything. Young people see themselves living in this world and it is their life yet to be lived.

Maya Angelou, American poet, writer, and entertainer

ⓖ　　ⓖ　　ⓖ

Grandparents, like heroes, are as necessary to a child's growth as vitamins.

Author unknown

Grandparents show children the mountaintops, while parents must teach them the drudgeries of how to get there.

T. Berry Brazelton, M.D., American pediatrician and child-development expert

I'm going to ask something of every one of you. . . . Let me start with my generation— the grandparents out there. You are our living line to the past. Tell your grandchildren the story of the struggle waged, at home and abroad. Of sacrifices freely made for freedom's sake. And tell them your own story as well—because every American has a story to tell.

George H. W. Bush, 41st president
of the United States

⑥　⑥　⑥

I think grandparents are more important than they ever were. With both parents working and the divorce rate rising, it's really critical for the grandparents to be there as a steady beacon for their grandchildren.

T. Berry Brazelton, M.D., American pediatrician and child-development expert

Grandparents are for saying, "I think you're okay."

Charlie W. Shedd, American writer

Most grandparents . . . try hard not to interfere. On the other hand, they have had experience, they feel they've developed judgment, they love their grandchildren dearly, and they can't help having opinions.

Benjamin Spock, M.D., American pediatrician and writer

6   6   6

The important things haven't changed, namely the presence of a grandparent in the life of a child, your presence in the life of your grandchildren.

Karen O'Connor, American writer

When grandparents enter the door, discipline flies out the window.

Ogden Nash, American poet

When a child talks to his great-grandparents, he can connect with as many as six generations—his own, his parents', his grandparents', and his great-grandparents', and through their firsthand accounts his great-great- and great-great-great-grandparents.

Perry Buffington, American psychologist and syndicated columnist

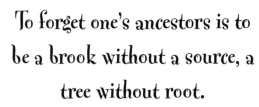

To forget one's ancestors is to be a brook without a source, a tree without root.

Chinese proverb

The great-grandparent serves at the trunk of the family tree.

Gregory Sanders, American educator

Grandparents are for telling you what it used to be like, but not too much.

Charlie W. Shedd, American writer

The closest friends I have made through life have been people who also grew up close to a loved and loving grandmother or grandfather.

Margaret Mead, American anthropologist and writer

(6)   (6)   (6)

Most people had good grandparents. And when they start talking about their grandmother's cooking or the place their grandparents lived, their eyes go soft. Their voices soften. They remember it as a safe house, a calm, quiet place in the universe.

Mary Pipher, American writer

Grandparents are people who come to your home, spoil the children, and then go home.

Author unknown

to grandpa

My parents were always telling me to hurry up; my grandparents were always telling me to slow down.

Author unknown

Grandparents are our continuing tie to the near-past, to the events and beliefs and experiences that so strongly affect our lives and the world around us.

Jimmy Carter, 39th president
of the United States

Grandparents should be one of a child's most valuable resources.

John Rosemond, American family psychologist
and syndicated columnist

Grandparents need grandchildren to keep the changing world alive for them. And grandchildren need grandparents to help them know who they are and give them a sense of human experience in a world they cannot know. Here is a model of mutual learning across generations.

Margaret Mead, American anthropologist and writer

⟨ ⟨ ⟨

A grandparent is old on the outside but young on the inside.

Author unknown

Nobody can do for little children what grandparents can do. Grandparents sort of sprinkle stardust over the lives of little children.

Alex Haley, American writer